HARNESSING STRESS

HARNESSING STRESS

A Spiritual Quest

Susan Muto and Adrian van Kaam

Imprimatur: Most Reverend Donald William Wuerl
Bishop of Pittsburgh
September 17, 1993

Scripture selections are taken from the New American Bible.

First published in 1993 by Resurrection Press, Ltd.
P.O. Box 248
Williston Park, NY 11596

ISBN 1-878718-18-5

Cover design and photograph by John Murello

Printed in the United States of America.

Contents

Introduction 7

1. **Coping with Conflict as a Challenge to Change** 9

2. **Creative Conflict Advances Our Spiritual Quest** 14

3. **Harnessing Stress through Conflict Resolution** 18

4. **The Laser Beam of Stress Attention** 22

5. **Developing Stress Attention** 28

6. **Keeping Distress in Check** 34

7. **Seeking Ways to Harness Stress before It Harms Us** 40

8. **Stress Tolerance in Labor and Leisure** 46

9. **Harnessing Stress to Deepen Spiritual Living** 49

10. **Coming to Inner Rest in the Midst of Stress** 53

Conclusion 56

Bibliography 59

Introduction

In the first book of this Spirit Life Series on stress and spirituality, we strove to show that stress as normally experienced in everyday life does not have to retard our search for happiness. To the contrary, it can actually enhance it. There, in addition to giving a general overview of stress, we presented some basic obstacles and conditions for living wisely in accordance with the invitations and challenges inherent in our here and now situation.

In the initial chapters of this second book we will show that stress plays a role, for better or worse, in any conflict situation. We will examine this dynamic of daily life from many angles, for it is like a tiger that has to be tamed if it and the stress it evokes are to advance our quest for a mature spiritual life in the light of Christ.

The remaining chapters of the book will be devoted to exploring concrete ways in which we can harness stress and make it, so to speak, the "lead horse" on our spiritual quest.

We will see just how important it is to rein in conflict, stress, and tension, bodily, emotionally, and spiritually. These movements affect for better or worse the way we feel, the way we function, and the way we live our faith.

Before we begin, we would like to thank two special people who reduced our stress considerably by helping us in the concrete production of these texts, Marilyn Russell, our administrative assistant, and Karen Holttum, our expert typist.

1

Coping with Conflict as a Challenge to Change

Life without the healthy stress of conflict is unthinkable. Conflict in itself need not lead to distress. The question is how do we handle conflicts, not how do we get rid of them? It goes without saying that there is a normal quotient of stress that accompanies every conflict.

A can opener that will not work arouses in us conflicted feelings of aggravation and irritation. What kind of workmanship would produce such an inferior instrument? We feel cheated out of good money and resent having to return this product to its place of purchase.

Our sense of conflict rises proportionately when the tension we feel is not between us and a broken utensil but between two people in a breakable, if not already broken, relationship.

The strain of conflict is felt in both of these situations, to be sure. Yet it need not be assumed that conflict as such is an obstacle to living a healthy and happy life in tune with the peace Christ gives to us.

Our faith assures us that the Holy Spirit will show us how to harness conflicted situations before they make us feel helpless. Stress can be an opening to gaining new insight into self and others. The grace of God seems to be sparked by conflict. It challenges us to seek creative ways of wisely managing and eventually transcending all negative stress.

Embracing the Cross of Conflict

Coping with conflict presupposes that we acknowledge the stress we are feeling. We must not deny how aggravated we are due to the strain and tension inherent in conflicted situations and relations. We need to ask ourselves if we are willing to embrace the cross of conflict as a call to grow in fidelity to the will of the Father as Jesus did (cf. Mt 26:42; Lk 22:42; and 23:46).

We see in Jesus' life that conflict is inseparable from growth. His friendship with Peter, Peter's betrayal, and Jesus' forgiveness of him are illustrative of how fully the Word of God entered into our conflicted human condition (cf. Mt 16:13–20; 26:69–75; and Jn 21:15–19).

The danger is that we might want to stop all conflict instead of flowing with it. We may think that doing away with conflict will automatically diminish stress. Nothing could be farther from the truth. Conflict is an indicator of the mystery, not a problem to be mastered. In the midst of strife and tension there are some formative questions we need to ask. One of these is: Do I allow conflict to disrupt unduly my ability to center my life in the Lord? If it feels as if we are crumbling under excessive strain, is this not an occasion to examine the depth and quality of our spiritual life? Another question conflict evokes is, therefore, how weak or strong is my faith?

Such questions as these lead to the conclusion that we must change the way we view the connection between conflict and stress. Rather than negatives, we must recognize these events and emotions as guides to positive, productive living. Would a pianist who never felt the stress of practice be able to interpret one of Bach's compositions? Would a marriage where the couple never had any honest battles but always put anger on the backburner not be in danger of exploding and breaking apart?

Conflict can press us down if we let it — like a steam roller over cement. It can depress us and certainly place us under severe stress. Still we have to believe that something beautiful can be composed under pressure.

From Collision to Creation

When we walk past the window of a fine jewelry store, we are struck by the beauty of the opals, sapphires, and diamonds glittering in the light. We can only imagine the forces and pressures of nature that produced them over eons of time.

Think of the cataclysmic forces that end in an earthquake or a volcanic eruption.

To us these forces may seem only disastrous, but every conflict in nature has a purpose. Some of the richest mineral beds in the world are located on the fiercest terrains. For thousands of years the collisions in the crust of the earth put deeply buried matter under enormous stress, yet it was this very pressure that changed once inert minerals into exquisite gems.

By analogy, we could say that the divine-forming mystery we call God invites us through the collision courses of daily life to become a new creation (cf. 2 Cor 5:17). Conflict is not only an invitation to grow; it is a challenge to change. It points to relations that are damaging and irreconcilable from which one has to disentangle, as in the case of physical or psychological abuse, as well as to relations that have every chance to blossom if people are willing to undergo the pruning process grace always guides.

When we least expect it, we may experience the creative side of conflict and actually welcome the stress that it places us under. Those are the times when our adrenalin begins to flow. We know that we have to pass through the tunnel of healthy conflict to reach the field of happiness on the other side.

Transcending Tension

There is no doubt that we feel the stress of conflict at such moments more than its creative potential. We have much to appraise, and this takes time, patience, and energy. We have many questions to consider, such as, is what we want in tune with what God wants us to do or suffer?

At times it feels as if a tug of war is going on inside of us between our pride form and our Christ form, between demonic spirits and the Holy Spirit. Depending on the seriousness of the situation, on how close it touches upon fidelity to our life call, we feel acutely conflicted.

On the one hand, we are only too aware of our desires for this or that outcome; on the other hand, something inside us, our reason inspired by faith, tells us what we ought to pursue. The resolution of such conflicts rests upon the graced transcendence of these either/or tensions.

When we move away from the apparent dilemma — which any conflict initially evokes — and try to see the wider picture, we often find a compromise solution. We can then enjoy the best of both worlds. The "Serenity Prayer" says it so well: "God grant me the serenity to accept the things I cannot change, the courage to change the things I can, and the wisdom to know the difference."

2

Creative Conflict Advances Our Spiritual Quest

We can diminish the distress evoked by conflict if we realize that it is not a contest. Rather than working directly at trying to dissolve the stresses of conflict or trying to excise their causes, it is wiser to use our time and energy to turn this seeming source of distress into an opportunity to deepen the divine gift of happiness and harmony God wants for us. How does this happen?

As we shall see, stress does not have to hinder our search for a happy, grace-filled life with Christ as long as we harness it wisely. God wants to give us the gift of lasting peace and joy. This is the goal of our spiritual quest, but we have to be willing to receive it. We have to listen to the invitation of the Spirit to look beyond mere limits and conflicts to an horizon of meaning waiting to disclose itself.

We have to be convinced that there is a way to embrace and effectively include in our life call the grain of consonance in every experience of conflict. We have to wager that some good can come out of the tension we are experiencing with any person, situation, or thing.

We and those with whom we are in conflict have to be willing to rise above the strains and tensions that might otherwise destroy us. We have to accept that all of us are wounded, that no one is totally perfect, that we all have room to grow. The alternative — to hold on to the conflict and seek revenge rather than resolution — is bound to be destructive.

Coping with Conflict

Looked at this way, we can say that conflict offers us a unique occasion to grow in the life of the spirit. It helps us to become more compatible with others, more compassionate with their and our own vulnerability, more patient and flexible, less willful or will-less.

In this way, we may come to accept as normal the field of stress that surrounds the minor and major conflicts and crises that are inseparable from living.

Coping with conflict is exactly what leads us to become wise and strong. As the old saying goes, the untried life is not worth living. Added to this adage is our conviction that life without conflict and stress never moves beyond adolescence. The spiritual maturity associated with adult Christian living has to pass through the test of fire and still survive.

We do not hold that conflict does not sting. We do hold

that it has to be accepted with courage and appreciated as a challenge sent by God to prevent us from succumbing to the complacency of a life that remains as weak and flabby as an unexercised body. Without such tests of mature living, we may die spiritually long before we die physically.

Attaining Stress Tolerance

To cope with conflict maturely, we have to occasionally test the degree of stress tolerance we have thus far reached. It is important to become aware of the caliber of increased or decreased endurance of stress. We have to be fine tuned to its ebb and flow. We have to catch the signs of excessive tension and immediately move toward a more transcendent stance.

As this happens we will be able to spot more quickly pockets of anger and aggression, especially when we are suddenly or unexpectedly exposed to the stress of conflict. We have to see it less as a hindrance and more as a help, however veiled, in our quest for spiritual maturity.

One can only speculate on how many marriages could have been saved if couples had had the know-how and the courage to harness the forces of stress.

Once we name, for example, our anger, we can move to identify more precisely the deformed feelings, thoughts, dispositions, or directives that evoked it in the first place. Real reformation begins to take place. The moment may come when we see clearly and calmly that if we do not make the move toward transcendence, the conflicts we are experiencing will bury us under an avalanche of distress.

Now is the time to distance ourselves from the epicenter of the conflict and to ask God to grant us the grace of inner calm. We pray that the God who loves us will turn this onslaught of depreciative emotions into an occasion to renew and refine our ability to become creative, not in spite of conflict but because of it.

We can almost feel the tension quotient subsiding at this time. We are no longer afraid to walk through the fire of stress because we know it will purify our heart and bring us closer to the cross of Christ. Conflict will become a graced opportunity to work out our salvation.

In upcoming chapters of this book, we will show how this is possible. For now it is enough to say that we must befriend the pain God's providence allows in our life if we want to become the new creations God intends us to be.

3

Harnessing Stress through Conflict Resolution

Where is our spiritual quest leading us? That is the question. From all that we have said thus far, it is clear that stress is not an invincible obstacle to our living a happy life but an inspiring challenge. We have to learn to rise above the issues that lead to our withdrawal from God and from one another. Pulling away from grace always results in a stressful life. We have to learn to appraise the thoughts, images, and feelings that give rise to little caverns, if not whole craters, of tension between us.

Our goal is thus to advance beyond the narrow focus of an overstressed, conflicted life, counterproductive of peace. We have to come to a wider vision of how God sees us, our life and our world. We have to ask continually what Christ would do or say in such a situation.

This awareness of our relationship to God will set us on the road to the resolution of unhealthy strife. If we take this path, risky as it may be, we will discover a whole range of possibilities for growth and maturity in ourselves and others. Life will be more like an open than a closed window. Mutual understanding will replace the misery of misunderstanding.

We can and must find a way to let stress sustain rather than destroy our togetherness. Creatively coping with conflict does not mean that we should concede submissively that we are wrong. Conflict resolution is not about groveling. If we are right, we have to stick by our story while striving gently yet firmly to restore lost harmony.

Such negotiation is always a more mature response to conflict than blind concession or fearful capitulation. These immature ways out of conflict cover up, they do not remove, the pain of normal stress. Sooner or later we have to face into the storm if we are to enjoy the calm that comes after it.

Reconciling Our Relationships

Before we can resolve our disagreements, we must agree to disagree agreeably. We are, after all, persons working toward the same cooperative end. Reconciliation draws us to a more transcendent plane. From this perspective, as from no other, we may behold a resolution that has thus far eluded us. Such an agreement would have been impossible had we not taken the long road of working through conflict and harnessing stress rather than allowing it to work on us destructively.

Against the background of regained harmony and the reduction of the tension, issues once heatedly debated may not seem so irreconcilable. What seemed only to tear us apart may now be seen as a normal part of the process of growing together. We try to create a liveable, if not loveable, compromise — knowing that such a way is possible only if we allow Christ to come between us and to hold our hands.

Now we are able to praise God for giving us the gifts of stress, tension, and conflict, for they gave us a golden opportunity to come to know one another on a new level. We may have a few scars, but we are now more able to see the stars.

Gift of Respect for One Another in Christ

Our spiritual quest has to be dynamic. It ought never to grow static in the putrid air of complacency. It ought to deepen our togetherness amidst the strifes and stresses of daily relationships. God calls us through it all to share in the goodness, truth, and beauty meant for us from the beginning. It is not so hard for us to bear with our differences and tensions when we are all being invited to share the same banquet.

God did not create us in isolation. He connected us to one another as members of the same family in the Mystical Body of Christ (cf. Rom 12:4–8 and 1 Cor 12:12–31). For this reason alone we should strive to resolve our conflicts. We should diminish the tensions that despoil the togetherness intended for us as brothers and sisters in Christ, who call God "Abba," "Father" (cf. Gal 4:6–7).

Respect for the unique life call of every man, woman, and child on earth is a Christian ideal. Such respect needs to be shown especially to those who cause us stress. This will guarantee that we do not lose our capacity for loving appreciation of all people, even when many around us have succumbed to the destructive power of depreciation.

We need to foster respectful love for self and others with God at the center. This disposition more than any other can help us to maintain our peace amidst the normal tugs and tensions felt on the path to human togetherness.

Jesus' gift of peace, his farewell gift to us (cf. Jn 14:27), is the tie that binds inspired people to one another. It is a symbol of the coming reign of God, a taste of the heaven of happiness awaiting us already here on earth. It is a gift worth striving for, no matter how stressful our lives may feel at the moment.

If we can harness the normal stress surrounding conflict like a force field around a power station, it can become a source of self-insight and creativity. In fact, without conflict and stress our spiritual quest cannot be effective.

4

The Laser Beam of Stress Attention

To prevent stress from becoming distress out of touch with the presence of Jesus is the goal of a Christ-centered life.

Stress becomes distress if we add to the normal conflicts and challenges of daily life self-centered, anxious expectations of what ought to be. We tense up when things do not go our way, when our best laid plans go astray.

Imagine that your boss asks you unexpectedly to come to his private office. You feel anxious. This is normal. However, what if a truckload of concerns rolls in at the same time? "Does this mean I'm getting a pink slip? Am I dressed properly for the occasion?"

Image upon image, fearful thought upon fearful thought, rush in and disrupt a calmer frame of mind. These ifs and buts may overwhelm you. They push stress over the edge of reasonableness into the white waters of distress. This is especially likely to happen if temperamentally your stress tolerance happens to be on the low side.

We could apply this typical case to countless other examples. All are linked by the common bond of daily life and the way it exposes us, like it or not, to a wide range of potentially distressful situations. Handling these is essential if we are to harness stress and make it a productive part of our spiritual quest.

Directing Our Attention

Many self-help and other books contain a variety of practical suggestions to alleviate the stress factor. Some of this counsel is useful to us, and we shall present it in the chapters to come. Here we need to ask ourselves if there is a preferable means of stress reduction. Is there one way that undergirds all the other practical counsels we can find to harness stress?

We believe there is such a basic way. You will easily recognize it. We all have access to it. Though we rarely use it, it is always available to us. Its name is "attention." We do not mean paying attention to a lesson here or an idea there but being attentive all the time to what is going on within our own hearts and minds. This attention has to be ongoing. It has to be the foundation of our continuing spiritual formation. It is a practice and a process that will be with us for a lifetime. It is our greatest aid to stress reduction and stress tolerance.

Analogy to a Laser Beam

At times this way of attention will be at the forefront, at other times in the background, of our comings and goings. We could compare this gift of ongoing attention to a laser beam. Most of us have probably heard of the medical breakthroughs associated with the use of lasers in some surgical procedures. Operations that used to keep people in the hospital for days can now be done on an out-patient basis.

A laser is a device in which light waves are so amplified and concentrated that they can be sharply focused. This technique gives rise to a narrow, intense beam whose enormous power can cut away tumors and other impurities in one fell swoop without harming surrounding healthy tissue.

Similarly, ongoing attention could be called the laser of the spirit. It helps us not only to scope out what is causing our stress but to find a way to cut it out. Mostly, we keep this spirit power in storage. When we do use it, even for a brief duration, it can have an excellent effect on the way we harness stress before it becomes harmful to us.

Formative Stress Reduction

A bit of surgery must take place where we need it most. We have to engage in a form of preventive medicine by becoming aware of the "harmful tissue" (self-centered, anxious or overly ambitious and perfectionistic ideas and decisions) and placing it under the powerful laser beam of our spirit-filled attention. Such sources of distress have to be excised, otherwise stressful emotions will get the best of us.

Good formation practice asks this attention of us. If we are unable to disclose what is causing us to feel so terrible, it will gain the upper hand before we know it. Thus we cannot escape paying attention if we want to grow.

We ought to tap into this resource for stress reduction not only during crisis moments but in the ordinary course of life. We shouldn't wait until we are in church or participating in a day of recollection or a retreat to start paying attention to what is going on in our bodies, minds, and hearts. We have to turn on the laser beam of attention as often as necessary to change abnormal stress back into the normal range of what is manageable for us.

Focusing on the Present

It is safe to say that our entire adult life should be an exercise in peaceful and pointed attentiveness. Nothing can help us as much as this to take in stride the ups and downs that often destroy people when they persist in living attention-dissipating rather than attention-gathering lives.

Spiritual formation requires that we be attentive to our unique-communal life call. There is a need for us to deal with the distress that causes us to detour from its direction. Being attentive to stress is the best thing we can do to harness the power of our calling and make it productive.

Think of what might happen were we to replay that scene with the boss. The message comes that we have to go to his office. Feeling stress starting up like an engine, we apply to it our laser beam of spirit-filled attention. It quickly removes distressful thoughts and images and attunes us to the here and now. We accept this disruption in our plans as an occasion to be attentively present to what is about to transpire and our inner reactions to it. It may mean that we have to face the challenge of seeking another position; it may mean some kind of promotion. We will only know the answer after we have gone into the meeting, listened to the communication, and had time to assess its contents on the spot or thereafter.

Undue Stress

The laser beam of attention shows us that we have to stop "crystal-balling" about the future and stay focused on the present. What complicates this simple process of "being present where we are" is undue distress. Overcoming it is not necessarily due to a lack of good will on our part. None of us really want to live this way. Our faith assures us that such a fractured life cannot be what Jesus intends for us.

The real problem may be that we are not sufficiently aware of the nagging, fantastic thoughts that lead to our anxiety-ridden perception of daily happenings. Attending to the waste products in the rummage barrel of distress will free our formation energy to deal with minor or major difficulties and to see the difference between them.

Counselors, true friends, and spiritual guides may suggest at what point we are going off the track. It is good to listen to their counsel. However, no one can tell us in exact detail how, when, and where we become unwitting victims of the "demons" of introspectionistic, fearful rumblings that generate — as an active volcano does molten lava — unnecessary stress that affects adversely all that we think about, do, and suffer.

Is this not one of the reasons why so few people can profit lastingly from the reading they amass about stress? These rules do not hit home. They cannot be remembered unless we have put to continuous use our laser beam of stress attention in the light of the Gospel. We need to ask the Holy Spirit to cultivate in us this distinctively human power granted to us by the Creator. It will help us to understand our vulnerability in this regard — to flow with it rather than to fight against it.

5

Developing Stress Attention

One condition that enables us to develop effective stress attention is to catch the kite-tail of an unrealistic fantasy life. We have to rein in such mind-spinning flights. They cause us to soar on the air currents of images and ideas that are soon out of touch with the demands of life and its normal quotient of stress.

Such "flying high" gives rise to exhausting, fantastic inventions that block realistic thinking. We subtly refuse to deal soberly with reality. We build a fantasy life that pretends to diminish stress but in the end only places us under the discomfort of distress.

Stress of a Fantasy Life

All of us, whether we admit it or not, spend a considerable amount of time and energy fantasizing about this or that relationship, event, or thing. Any stressful moment can trigger this wish-fulfillment mechanism. Sometimes its true nature is camouflaged by calling it clever analysis of all that may happen to us. Wise, graced analysis in the light of the spirit of Jesus is nothing of the kind. It is reality-oriented.

Once again we need to pull out the laser beam of attention to blow away as quickly as possible these clouds of fantasy and come down to earth. Constant practice in this regard puts us back in touch with our quest for in-depth spiritual formation in Jesus. It enhances our chance to live a life centered in Christ that is relatively free from distress.

We could say that the mark of a life that is not overstressed is the serenity of Christ that gives forth energy. The opposite — a stress-filled existence chasing after elusive fantasies — is bound to be life-draining. It opens us to the Evil One who cannot take away our freedom but who will play on our fantasy life, to be sure.

Many people live by the mistaken notion that to rid oneself of distressing flights of fancy demands a long and arduous process. The contrary is true. Rather than diving again into the rummage barrel of "what-ifs" and "if onlys," it is better to try the opposite tactic.

If we try to escape the trap of anxious fantasy by dealing with it head on, it will entrap us. Such willfulness feeds into our pride form, which is the nourishing ground of our self-centered fantasies. The same happens in meditation. If we try to diminish our distractions directly, we may find that this effort itself distracts us even more. The best thing we can do is to be attentive to that about which we are meditating — a prayer, a scripture text, a line from a poem. The more we pay attention to it, the less distractions will detract our thoughts from the "more than."

If we allow ourselves to get lost in the labyrinth of obsessive fantasies, thinking more about them than about the Divine Will here and now, we will never be free from the maze. It will only expand its winding paths and false starts until we lose our way entirely.

Halting Fantasy to Alter Distress

To escape this predicament and its hampering of our true spiritual quest, we must be present to the fact that we are caught in fantasy-thoughts again. Then we have to say immediately, "Enough is enough, dear Lord. This is not the way I want to go. Stop it."

It helps immensely for us Christians to focus at such moments on the warm and welcoming face of Christ. Look into his eyes. They will guide you home. Listen to the voice of the Spirit within. Then you will hear the gentle invitation to return to the path God calls you to follow in the here and now in accordance with his inviting and challenging will. Then you will not feel alone in this endeavor. You can let go of the crutch of wish-filled fantasies and cling to the hands of Christ. Then your command to halt distress turns into a prayer.

Holy Spirit, strengthen my stress attention. Give me inner eyes to see my deviation from the reality of God's will for my life at this time. Divine Master, halt this obsessive string of fantasies as soon as I ask you this favor. Instill in me absolute trust in your timetable for my life. Let me count my blessings and not worry about useless fantasies that erode my faith and my fidelity to your will here and now.

In this way we rid ourselves, with the aid of grace, of endless weavings that produce undue stress. By relaxed yet persistent, gentle yet firm, observation of these inner thought processes, we begin to recognize as in a new light how much energy we have wasted in self-preoccupied concerns and their stressful by-products.

The more we grow over the years in this kind of letting go, the more we let the power of the Holy Spirit sustain our human capacity to harness stress as a means to foster our spiritual quest. By thus diminishing the distress that comes through imagination-run-wild, we can find ways to channel our stress creatively as Christ himself did.

Spiritual Stress Management

Humanly speaking, Jesus had to have felt his stress quotient rise at the wedding feast of Cana when he was told that the stewards were running out of wine. He addressed this real situation in a remarkable way that was in keeping with his obedience not only to his mother's request but to his call to begin his public life (cf. Jn 2:1–11).

This kind of spiritual stress management implies that we focus diligently on the situation in which we find ourselves called and challenged and let our fantasies about it fall by the wayside.

What is, is. What is right, is right. What is wrong, is wrong. Such clear-headedness is light years away from the muddied waters of mindless wandering. We are no longer caught by the net of distress and dragged along in it as helpless fish. Redeemed from the distressing impact of fantasy thoughts on our inner life, we sense what it means to be liberated by the power of the Risen Christ. He lifts us from the mire of obsessive wishes into the clear mountain air of freedom from distress.

Following the Way of the Lord

We must cooperate with Christ in this venture of liberation. He wants us to develop our gifts of vigilance and attentiveness to the really real. Cleaning house, washing cars, going shopping, working at home or in the office—all these actions call for formation in realistic attention. We should be as lovingly attentive to the gift of the moment as Christ was to every person in need from the daughter of Jairus to the woman who touched his garment (cf. Mk 5:21–43).

In all that we do in Jesus' name, we are to be fully present with and in him to the will of the Father as revealed in the task at hand. This is our duty. This is our responsibility. When it is time to work, we work. When it is time to play, we play. This simple rule applies to our every activity and relationship.

Normal stresses are hidden in all of these endeavors. We expect them. We do not overreact to them. We tune in to what they are teaching us. We stop in its tracks any fantasy that evokes distress subtly or dramatically.

Such thoughts may range from our having to be perfect to our being afraid. They will not get the best of us if we bring out our laser beam of spirit-filled attention and halt them with Christ's help.

It may even happen, as we move forward in our spiritual quest, that we come to welcome these normal stresses as signs of the cross Jesus wants us to carry for his sake (cf. Mk 8:34–35). To bear them in peace and joy enables us to walk with the Lord from Golgotha to the tomb from which he rose. Likewise there will arise in us in a whole new way the lustrous beauty of our Christ form that will free us from distress more than any advice or counsel we may seek.

6

Keeping Distress in Check

To tame the stress that tugs at our heart is not easy. It demands that we work toward some lifestyle changes that are at once disciplined and creative.

As we have seen, we need to live in attentiveness to the hidden thoughts that lurk in the background of our feelings of distress. To help initiate a course correction, ask Christ in simple honest words to help you diminish the intensity of the thoughts that disconcert you by changing the mental words and images that trigger them. Ask Jesus to make you aware of how you yourself evoke in others angry counter feelings because you do not treat them with kindness and consideration.

Often distress happens because our lifestyle has become increasingly aggressive or withdrawn, not at all in tune with Christ's example. Harnessing stress begins to happen when we allow the Holy Spirit to inspire us with the conviction that the time for change is now.

Reformation Redeems Distress

One basic motivation for such reformation of character should be the desire we feel in our heart of hearts to be more consonant with Christ. We know from the Gospel that his life was not marked, as ours sometimes is, by intense irritation, frustration, and rage. He showed calm stress control at highly charged emotional moments; he did not gripe, seek retribution, or pout.

We know also from the writings of the apostle Paul that our body is a temple of the Holy Spirit (cf. 1 Cor 3:16–17). God wants us to take good care of it. One way to stay healthy is to maintain our temple well. If God gives us the gift of health, and we do not abuse our body, we may be more effective instruments to serve God's reign on earth and to fulfill our unique part in a divine plan meant for us from all eternity.

Continuous distress, by contrast, may place us at a higher risk of physical or emotional illness. This lessens a special effectiveness God may have intended for us. We are to be instruments for transforming the world into the House of God. We are to use to the full the gifts and talents we have been given while welcoming the cross of our limitations.

Reinforcing Our Resolution to Reduce Stress

Make up your mind that it is time to change from being a frequently distressed person to one who can cope with normal stress creatively. Reinforce this resolve by telling yourself that you want to be, with the help of grace, a better parent, spouse, friend, teacher, student or professional. Are there easy-to-follow guidelines that help us to keep distress in check?

A first suggestion is to keep track of the thoughts that triggered your distress initially. Even saints like Thérèse of Lisieux kept a diary. Why not write — at least in the beginning — a kind of "distress log." Whenever you become aware that you are feeling distressed, name how and why you feel this way. Write down in your journal both the distress you felt and the thought that preceded or accompanied the upset. Write your entry in as prayerful a manner as possible.

If you happen to be with other people when the flare up occurs, wait a while and then later pen your entry. Be specific. Name the time and place. Identify what set in motion your distressing thoughts. What was the triggering event, person, conversation or situation? What thoughts stirred you up the most, the least? What feelings did you have? Did you take any action?

Logging your distress might be the best thing you can do to harness the depreciative power of stress before it hampers your spiritual quest.

Logging Stressful Situations

Let's say you're a volunteer in a local hospital. You bring refreshments to patients before bedtime. On the way home from your shift, you sense symptoms of distress rising in you. Were you writing in your log, the page might read like this:

Who: The last woman I served blew up at me. She griped bitterly about the inefficiency of the hospital and its staff.

Thoughts: Who needs this difficult lady at this time of the night? Doesn't she realize how tired I am?

Feelings: Irritation. Desire to tell her off or to leave her without a word.

Actions: I handed her the juice she wanted but in an abrupt way. I did not offer the small talk that usually cheers people up. Upon leaving the room, I frowned at her. I raised my eyebrows rather than smiling.

Recording such distressful experiences in your log will make you attentive to the number of times and the kinds of situations that trigger feelings, attitudes, and behaviors that upset you, often unnecessarily. In time you will come to see your profile of stress, its trigger points and the thoughts, feelings, and actions to which they give rise.

This simple exercise can help you to halt the stream of distress that drives you to the breaking point. It will teach you that you can harness stress and re-channel your energy in a more creative way.

Replaying the Stress Tape

What if the woman was a chronic complainer? Maybe her stress tolerance failed because she had a terrible day. She was sick after all. Instead of sinking into distress yourself, maybe you could have said a prayer for her, or treated her with the compassion of Christ, or applied the old adage you learned from your grandmother: that one gets a lot more out of people with honey than with vinegar. Think of how much better you would have felt walking out of that room had you smiled and tried to cheer her up, even if she did not respond. You would have harnessed your distress and channeled it in the direction of your desire to live a more Christian life, especially as a volunteer working with the sick.

From time to time you can peruse your stress log as you would a text and see what it has to teach you. It may surprise you to find that many, if not most, of the logged events are about small annoyances rather than dramatic happenings. You see that often you yourself were the cause of the angry reactions you received from others. Had you changed your tune in time, they would have probably changed theirs.

Little Stresses Hurt a Lot

This discovery confirms the findings of a study conducted by the psychologist Richard Lazarus and colleagues at the University of California at Berkeley. They came to the conclusion that the greatest toll from stress may come not from such dreadful events as divorce, the loss of employment, or similar major misfortunes. To the contrary, the most common cause of stress turns out to be minor yet frequent annoyances. This is the "stuff" out of which everyday life is made: getting stuck in a traffic jam; gaining a few unwanted pounds; having an argument with your spouse, your children, or your friends.

The team also discovered that such relatively unimportant hassles often have a more negative effect on one's health than do larger-scale traumas. The small stresses, the mosquitoes of life, often turn into distresses, persistent stings, because of the litany of thoughts we have about them.

If we do not stop doing this to ourselves, the price we may have to pay is a case of high blood pressure, an asthma attack, chest pain, a stroke, ulcers, or flare-ups of arthritis. Those people congenitally vulnerable to such diseases are especially at risk.

Your log book can become a treasure of insight in this regard. It can complement your doctor's warning to avoid distress in your life along with other common risk factors. Most take that advice to mean: avoid big problems. If these are the big potatoes of life, then what we need to do is to pay attention to the chips that stick in our throats, that hassle us all the time. Research shows that these kinds of conflict have a deleterious effect on our physical, mental, emotional, and spiritual health. We have to keep them in check if we want to cooperate fully with the grace of transformation.

7

Seeking Ways to Harness Stress before It Harms Us

When we read the Gospel, we become aware of what a wonderful counselor Christ was. People like the paralytic at Capernaum could bring any sin to him for healing, any feeling of guilt, stress, or pain (cf. Mk 2:1–12). As a result, the causes of their distress came out of the closet of their closed off inner life and were brought into the light of God's love.

Such honest disclosures of the way it really is with us loosen the shackles of distress that cut us off from forgiveness when we most need it. We become more matter-of-fact about the sources of our distress. We tell it "like it is" to God, if not to a trusted other. Once such "secrets" are out in the open, in the healing ambiance of God's loving vision, we can deal with them more realistically.

Heartfelt confessions can draw over us like a warm blanket the sun of divine graces. Touched to the quick are those parts of our being and doing that have drawn us into an anxious, stressful existence that retards our quest for peace and joy.

If possible, we should not restrict our confession to God or to a priest or minister. We should seek help also from people whom we trust in daily life. For example, we can let our spouse or a close friend in on the "secret" that we know we have a problem handling stress wisely. Too often it becomes distress. Too often we feel as if we have to bear this burden alone.

Intimate Trust Relieves Tension

The confidante to whom we turn can support our efforts to change. Already this act of trusting intimacy with a person helps to relieve distress. You let this person see into you, trusting that he or she will continue to love you.

"Here's a person who is not put off by my imperfections but who cares for me all the more." Ask him or her to tell you when you are beginning to be ensnared again by the net of fantasy thoughts and the stressful effects they evoke. This honest communication seems to have a double effect for good when it comes from someone who has our well being at heart.

Immediate Response to Distress

We have seen that the main cause of irrational distress is any flight of anxious fantasy. We have to train ourselves to halt it. We need to ask the Lord to help us to harness distress immediately. Unless we have mastered this one point, we risk obsessing about these "mosquitoes" so much so that their venom poisons our system continuously.

We may already know from our stress log what kinds of thoughts start the snowball rolling down the hill. This insight is itself a great grace. It helps us to get in touch sooner than later with these harmful thought patterns.

The outcome of this practice ought not to surprise us. The thoughts will stop. We release the blocked formation energy that anger and irritation used to cut short. Our whole life begins to flow in rhythm again with our Christ form. We repent with all sincerity that we have wasted so much energy on distress instead of investing it in fidelity to our divine life call. We realize in humility that the life we save may be our own.

Staying in Tune with Reality

Another way to harness stress is to use a "reality check." This limits our exaggerated chain of fantasy. To keep it in check, we need to ask if our feelings are really in proportion to the words or actions that triggered stress in the first place.

Are we perhaps inclined to exaggerate what happened or what we perceived took place? Do we attribute to the person who "ticked us off" motivations that are not really there? Do we read into the situation threats and dangers that are more the products of our anxious imagination than of what one can objectively observe?

Staying in Touch with the Present Moment

These checkpoints can be followed by what we might call a "time experience indicator." This means that we look with detachment at the past: *what was will not return;* with hope at the future: *what might be is in God's hands and God is good;* with faith at the present: *what is, the here and now, is what I have to work with.*

When our thoughts and feelings take off in unreasonable, unrealistic, fantastic flights, we may observe that we expend too much time "past-urizing" or "future-izing." We link so much of who we are to the past that we may color a here and now happening with every shade of the rainbow of past years or every unknown shadow of the future. The tiny slice of the present that evokes a bit of stress suddenly boils over into a thick soup of everything we ever did wrong and all we will never accomplish.

Instead of stress staying in touch with the present moment, it becomes like a huge sponge. It absorbs an ocean of past or anticipated future experiences. Trying to incorporate all of the past and all of the future with the events of today overwhelms and depresses us.

Here again we must halt and harness this misuse of formation energy by staying quietly in touch with what is: God's holy will in the here and now. We can ask the Lord to slow down our racing mind. We can say with the simplicity of a child: "The past is behind me. It cannot be retrieved or redone. The future is before me. It cannot be precisely predicted or controlled. My Lord has given me the gift of the present moment. Let me do with it what he wills. Let me see it as a sign of his love."

Diminishing Time Urgency

In dealing with the present, we have to check on one more important factor, the feeling of "time urgency." If we feel as if we never have enough time to do what has to be done, if we rush instead of walking, what does that mean? Are we failing once more to practice the presence of God?

"Time urgency" means that we are unable to be present to the always limited time we have to do anything. Instead of flowing gratefully and graciously with this minute or this hour, we try foolishly to push ahead of time. We feel an urgency to accomplish more than is possible in the frame of time given to us. We act as if there is never enough time to do anything.

Trying to push time faster than it goes is like trying to push a river. We forget that the river flows as it will. In this light the phrase "go with the flow" takes on new meaning. It becomes another way to harness anxious stress so that we can be open to the graces God sends that are always sufficient for the hour. Scripture tells us why we should not worry: "Seek first [God's] kingship over you, his way of holiness, and all these things will be given you besides. Enough, then of worrying about tomorrow. Let tomorrow take care of itself. Today has troubles enough of its own" (Mt 6:33–34).

Practicing the Power of Appreciation

One sure way to halt distress is to try to appreciate the good things around us. Do you take time to smell the roses, to laugh with friends, to celebrate meals together, and above all, to be with the Lord in prayer?

If we are honest about this, we may find to our dismay that we are often more depreciative than appreciative. We see the flaw in the marble rather than the loveliness of the artist's vision in stone.

Appreciation is a proven stress reducer. In fact, when we feel on the verge of making a cutting remark, try turning it into a compliment. Stress deflates at such moments like a spent balloon.

Our research has revealed two rules of thumb that enable us to harness stress before it harms us:

1. Depreciation gives rise to distress.
2. Appreciation puts us on the road to peace and joy.

Stress Tolerance in Labor and Leisure

If our stress tolerance is low, we tend to become tense about almost everything. Whether we are laboring at a project or enjoying a day of leisure, we feel strained for some reason. Our ease of heart and mind is at a low ebb. It is as much an effort to daydream as it is to make hard decisions. We also lose touch with the movements of the Spirit within. We find it difficult to connect what is happening to a Christian horizon of meaning where suffering and joy have their place on the journey homeward to God.

To the degree that we have failed to handle the challenge of distress, we will be less able to bear with normal stress. A wrong way to cope with the problem of low-stress tolerance is to push ourselves irrationally to accomplish something difficult, no matter the cost. We may begin to overwork to prove to ourselves that we can handle tension and not waste time.

The right answer might be to become more like good gardeners. Look at the way they handle plants. They know how much water and sun each seedling needs to grow. We, too, should learn to handle people, events, and things and the stresses they cause with a gentle hand. If we treat stresses like plants cropping up in the garden of our life, we will know what has to be cultivated for the harvest to appear. We will sense as well what has to be uprooted for the sake of preserving the fertility of the whole field.

Enhancing Our Tolerance

To build up stress tolerance, we have to become more open to the sunshine of God's grace guiding us in labor and leisure. Instead of resisting our limits and trying to do too much, we should let go of our feverish pace. We should stand back in admiration and appreciation of what God has wrought through us.

In times of prayer and participation, we can give ourselves over to the calming climate of a stress-tolerant lifestyle. We can put to rest the anxious urge to do more and more things in less and less time. By becoming more relaxed and distress-free, we become more effective in our work. Our creative output increases. We sleep more soundly. We eat more regularly. We relate more warmly. We pray more wholeheartedly.

Our level of stress tolerance enhances our capacity to live within the limits of time without feeling we never have enough of it. How do we befriend the fact that there are only so many hours in the day without becoming distressed by its quick passing?

We have to develop at one and the same time a disposition of abiding with what is while seeing in it a message about what has to be done or suffered. Abandonment to the mystery supports our abiding while presence to our call enhances our creativity.

The disposition of stress tolerance controls the greediness and aggressiveness of a merely functional life. Thus we enjoy the best of both worlds: we are calm and centered in Christ in the midst of productive endeavors, though life is turning and churning around us. We unite with him and through him we care for whatever task he has entrusted to us.

In a sense we enjoy leisure while we are at labor. We attend to the mystery in contemplation while we are acting on its behalf to better our world. The more tolerant of stress we become, the more we are able to be smooth channels for the outflow of the forming mystery in presence and action.

9

Harnessing Stress to Deepen Spiritual Living

Excessive stress is a signal from the Spirit that we have to calm down. We know from experience as well as from the medical profession that a more relaxed lifestyle, sparked by normal stress in accordance with our profile of limits and assets, is good for us. Notwithstanding this common sense advice, we believe that the best way to harness debilitating stress is to deepen our spiritual life.

Sometimes, for no apparent reason, we may find ourselves feeling anxious and tense. This surprises us because we have been trying to harness these feelings for a long time. We may not know what is upsetting us. The physical signs are there — stiffness in our neck and shoulders, cramped stomach muscles, sweaty palms. These bodily signals have no reason to lie. The question is: Do we listen to a persistent headache; a bout of low back pain; a tight, dry mouth?

If we run a tape of the past few days, we may find that

pressure has been building up for all kinds of reasons. Of most concern to us is the possible neglect of our prayer life. This should be the first, not the last, area we examine when excessive stress reappears in our life. With this neglect may come other symptoms like irritability and oversensitivity to any criticism. We could name many related causes of this expanding tension but decreased prayer time is the most serious.

Stress as a Pointer to the Transcendent

Once we acknowledge the tension we are under, once we accept that we need the healing presence of God, we may notice almost immediately a lessening of pressure. We allow God to alleviate the anxiety we are feeling. We do not hide from him any secret or known source of pain. We pray with and through our experience of stress. We let God's hand harness it for us.

As we lift our distress up to God, we alleviate isolated concentration on self. If we focus on ourselves alone, we risk becoming more anxious about our progress. Prayer rescues us from this kind of frenzy. We allow ourselves to be carried by God while we try to see what meaning this tension has in the light of our life call in Christ.

In this way stress becomes an occasion to deepen our spiritual quest rather than to set it on a detour that depletes energy and makes us depreciative. We see that tension as such is not undesirable. It can be a pointer to the transcendent. It tells us that we have to search anew for the purpose God has in mind for our life.

On the vital level, stress can be a sign that the body is mobilizing itself to cope with an emergency or to remind us of the need for repletion of energy through sleep and rest. Stress as a warning helps us to restore our energy in service of the Transcendent. Tension only becomes inappropriate when it becomes more prevalent in our life than presence to the Transcendent. If we operate continually under too much stress, we risk cutting our lifeline to God in prayer. No wonder we gasp for relief like fish out of water.

On the functional level, a basic attitude of calm helps to upgrade our efficiency. Spiritual living always results in giving. We enjoy seeing the fruits God may grant to our labor, especially when they are nurtured by creative stress rather than deadened by depleting distress.

A sign that we are on the road to spiritual living is our awareness of the restlessness acknowledged by St. Augustine, who said in the first chapters of his *Confessions* that our hearts are restless (or spiritually stressed and stretched) until we rest in God.

Calming the Storm of Distress

From this perspective, we might say that our life in this world is a stretching toward the unattainable. That always creates in us a certain tension. Without this tension, we would neither know the Transcendent nor would we long to pass over into the Infinite.

Though we are nourished by the word of God, our hunger for this word can never be satisfied in this life. The far horizon open to eyes of faith ought not to terrify us; it ought to draw us on. If we are distracted from what eye has not seen and ear has not heard (cf. 1 Cor 2:9–10) by the storms of distress, we can ask God to calm the waters of our fears as he calmed the Sea of Galilee (cf. Mk 4:35–41).

Resistance and refusal of the Spirit obscure the vision Christ has for our life. The worst effect of distress is that it can block our trust in God. It is as if we erect a fence between us and what God most wants us to be. If we bend in the direction of the wind of grace, it will break down the fence, rescue us from the desert of distress, and move us toward the final stretch of our spiritual quest.

10

Coming to Inner Rest in the Midst of Stress

Though we may have been shackled by the chains of distress, we now let God remove them from our wrists. Spiritual writers like Augustine and Teresa of Avila speak of having a core of inner peace in the midst of outer agitation. They hold to the Christian ideal of our remaining recollected in the midst of work. Neither would say this balance is easy to attain, but at least we are on the way.

How can we be at peace inwardly while outwardly we are over-loaded with work and responsibility? The activities of modern life can reach whirlwind proportions as we know so well. Look at the faces of people rushing through airports or trying to shop and babysit at the same time.

The distress of nervous strain is written all over our bodies. We are aware when energy seeps out of us like ointment from a spent tube. The direction our life takes feels unsteady. We know that if we do not harness the horses of this push-and-pull type of existence, our life will run away from us like a team out of control.

Taking a walk in the evening or talking our agitation over with a friend can complement steady presence to God in prayer and sustain the gift of peace. We need these times of physical and emotional recollection to keep our lives in tune with Christ's inviting and challenging call to live as faithful servants, as witnesses to the fullness of love.

Refocusing on the Lord

Now is the time to ask ourselves if we have lost our point of focus, our center in the Lord. Without making one more excuse, fix your gaze on Christ. See him as the fountainhead of calming union for which you long. Look within yourself and you will find God waiting for you. Offer the Lord the prayer of your heart, saying:

> *Create space in me to gather in and calm down the circles of anxious activity in which I feel so dispersed. Let me see my involvements in the light of your providential plan for my life. For the sake of inner peace, help me to let go of all unnecessary concerns.*

Praying for Peace

Such pauses for prayer may show us that the cause of our agitation is a shift from God as center to self as center. Only the Lord can lay to rest our distress. Peace is God's sheltering gift, it is the key to fulfilling our life call in equanimity.

In the midst of distress, we can turn to God as trusting children and ask prayerfully for the gift of his peace (cf. Jn 14:27). It is good every evening to bring the agitation of our day before him and to pray that in the morning we will have the courage to continue our work. It is good to say, "All is in your hands, O Lord. Whether I succeed or fail, let your will, not mine, be done."

Such words gave people like Dag Hammarskjöld and Fr. Walter Ciszek the courage to carry their work to conclusion, even if they would not live to see the fruits of their efforts. Wherever we are and whatever we do, it is never too late to change our tune if it becomes disobedient or depreciative. When the words "I will" become "Thy will," we may cease asking God, "Why me?" and instead invite God to "Try me," in accordance with his graced and holy will for our lives.

Conclusion

Having harnessed our stress with the help of grace, having allowed stress to prompt our spiritual quest, it is time to pray with hearts on fire:

Lord, along the river bank the reeds of the marshlands are tossed and ruffled by the wind. How often I have watched storms blow in with their towering forces and batter the unprotected reeds to the ground in a flurry of wind and rain. Yet, when the wind dies down and I stroll by water's edge, I am amazed at the triumph of these fragile plants. Then I know the truth of your promise that the bruised and broken reed you will not scorn (cf. Is 42:3).

There they are, there am I, upright and strong in the morning breeze. How can a reed bend so low and not break? Your care fills me with awe. I see that below the surface of my stress, in the silent depths of your love, my life is secure. When the wind blows the strongest and the rains beat the hardest, the roots of my faith in you go so deep that I will not waver.

Lord, at times I think of myself as a wind-tossed reed. I find the world a stormy place. My employers are demanding, my colleagues deceptive, all my best efforts seem to be aborted. I feel miserable in the face of defeat, hurt by a lack of understanding, levelled like the reed by powers that threaten me on all sides. I become harsh with myself and with others. I want to whip my foolishness into shape. All I succeed in doing is to become more and more agitated, filled with self-depreciation and bitter feelings toward others.

Left to myself in the midst of distress I close my eyes and think of you. You tell me that though I am afraid, if I have faith, I shall find in the core of my being your peace.

You have made me a unique person. Though the contribution I have to make is limited, it is my unrepeatable offering of self through you to the world.

Your peace comes over me. In this moment of inwardness, I recognize anew the value of being who I am. I open my eyes to the world again. I am erect like a reed, at peace with myself and with you. From this inner peace flows a new-found readiness to reach out to others.

I have found more than my "self" in this inner core. Below the troubles of my mind and its emotional up-

surges, I descend into the spiritual center of my soul. It is difficult to get there, but I allow myself to slip down, to let go . . . knowing that in the sacred core of my being I am held and sustained by a tender hand.

Here, at a level below agitation, I am encompassed by you. In the infinite stillness which surrounds me, agitation disappears. In the peace of this moment, muscles relax; my mind is free of preoccupying thoughts; the whole of me is enveloped in the sustaining power of your peace. You have harnessed my stress, given me rest, and sent me into the world to do my best in your name. Amen.

Bibliography

Anderson, Robert A. *Stress Power! How To Turn Tension into Energy.* New York: Human Sciences Press, 1978.

Augustine, St. *The Confessions of St. Augustine.* Trans. John K. Ryan. Garden City, NY: Doubleday, Image Books, 1960.

Ciszek, Walter, S.J., with Daniel L. Flaherty. *He Leadeth Me.* Garden City, NY: Doubleday, 1973

Cousins, Norman. *The Healing Heart.* New York: Avon Books, 1983.

Friedman, Howard S. *Hostility, Coping & Health.* Washington, DC: American Psychological Association, 1992.

Hammarskjöld, Dag. *Markings.* Trans. Leif Sjöberg and W. H. Auden. New York: Alfred A. Knopf, 1969.

Muto, Susan. *Pathways of Spiritual Living.* Petersham, MA: St. Bede's, 1991.

______. *Renewed at Each Awakening: The Formative Power of Sacred Words.* Denville, NJ: Dimension Books, 1979.

______. *Womanspirit: Reclaiming the Deep Feminine in Our Human Spirituality.* New York: Crossroad, 1991.

______ and Adrian van Kaam. *Commitment: Key to Christian Maturity.* New York: Paulist Press, 1989.

———. and Adrian van Kaam. *Tell Me Who I Am.* Denville, NJ: Dimension Books, 1977.

Padus, Emrika. *The Complete Guide to Your Emotions & Your Health.* Emmaus, PA: Rodale Press, 1986.

Piddington, Ralph. *The Psychology of Laughter.* New York: Gamut Press, 1963.

Segal, Jeanne. *Living Beyond Fear.* New York: Ballantine Books, 1984.

Saràson, Irwin and Charles Spielberger. *Stress and Anxiety, Volume 1.* Washington, DC: Hemisphere Publishing Corporation, 1975.

——— and Charles D. Spielberger. *Stress and Anxiety, Volume 2.* Washington, DC: Hemisphere Publishing Corporation, 1975.

——— and Charles D. Spielberger. *Stress and Anxiety, Volume 3.* Washington, DC: Hemisphere Publishing Corporation, 1975.

Sehnert, Keith W. *Stress/Unstress: How You Can Control Stress at Home and on the Job.* Minneapolis: Augsburg Publishing House, 1981.

Teresa of Avila, St. *The Collected Works.* Trans. Kieran Kavanaugh, O.C.D., and Otilio Rodriguez, O.C.D. Washington, DC: Institute of Carmelite Studies, 1976.

Thérèse of Lisieux. *The Autobiography of St. Thérèse of Lisieux: The Story of a Soul.* Trans. John Beevers. Garden City, NY: Doubleday, Image Books, 1957.

van Kaam, Adrian. *Living Creatively.* Denville, NJ: Dimension Books, 1972.

———. *Music of Eternity: The Everyday Sounds of Fidelity.* Notre Dame, IN: Ave Maria Press, 1990.

———. *Religion and Personality.* Pittsburgh, PA: Epiphany Books, 1991.

______. *The Transcendent Self: Formative Spirituality of the Middle, Early, and Late Years of Life.* Pittsburgh, PA: Epiphany Books, 1991.

______ and Susan Muto. *Am I Living a Spiritual Life?* Denville, NJ: Dimension Books, 1978.

______ and Susan Muto. *The Power of Appreciation.* New York: Crossroad, 1993.

High quality, inexpensive, small books which promote Christian lifestyles in contemporary settings.

YOUNG PEOPLE AND . . . YOU KNOW WHAT
Eroding the New Paganism, *by William O'Malley, S.J.*

— For teachers, parents, youth ministers —

Bill O'Malley knows young people — he's been teaching them for over 30 years — and he knows how difficult it is to speak to them about sex. In this book he provides ways — using reason alone — to outfox teenage convictions that sex has no human consequences.

"When dealing with sex questions, parents and teachers have to be extraordinarily patient — and loving. . . . We are fighting against an Enemy who has been entrenched within their minds and value systems since they were sitting in their Pampers in front of the Electronic Babysitter."

ISBN 1-878718-13-4 40pp. **$3.50**

A powerful sequel to the bestselling Miracle Hour

5-MINUTE MIRACLES
Praying for People with Simplicity and Power, *by Linda Schubert*

"A gift to the Church today. . . . Linda Schubert has undoubtedly birthed a second miracle! A must read for all who desire to comfort others by praying with them and for those who have not yet dared to desire."

— Babsie Bleasdell

"Not just a gem, but a treasure-trove of inspiration. . . . Linda Schubert demonstrates that arm-around-the-shoulder informality plus let's-pray-about-it compassion can draw five-minute miracles from a God of incandescent love." — John H. Hampsch, C.M.F.

LINDA SCHUBERT is the author of *Miracle Hour,* which has sold over 300,000 copies, and is a worldwide speaker on the power of prayer.

ISBN 1-878718-08-8 64pp. **$3.95**

FAITH MEANS: If Your Pray for Rain, Bring an Umbrella
by Antoinette Bosco

"Antoinette Bosco has taken a mysterious subject — faith — and made it clear and comprehensible. Readers of all ages will finish this little book feeling both challenged and reassured." —Joan Wester Anderson

ANTOINETTE BOSCO is a syndicated columnist for *Catholic News Service* and the author of five books.

ISBN 1-878718-15-0 48pp. **$3.50**

NOTHING BUT LOVE: Health and Holiness through Intimacy with God
by Robert E. Lauder

"Sensitively and simply, Father Lauder deals with some of the most profound and mysterious aspects of Christian life: spirituality, prayer and especially the personal presence of God in people's lives. *Nothing but Love* should help many come into closer relationship with the God revealed in Jesus." —Bernard Cooke

ROBERT LAUDER is a professor of philosophy at St. John's University in Jamaica, NY and the author of eight books.

ISBN 1-878718-16-9 64pp. **$3.95**

Spirit-Life Audiocassette Collection

Witnessing to Gospel Values *Paul Surlis*	$6.95
Celebrating the Vision of Vatican II *Michael Himes*	$6.95
Hail Virgin Mother *Robert Lauder*	$6.95
Praying on Your Feet *Robert Lauder*	$6.95
Annulment: Healing-Hope-New Life *Thomas Molloy*	$6.95
Life After Divorce *Tom Hartman*	$6.95
Path to Hope *John Dillon*	$6.95
Thank You Lord! *McGuire/DeAngelis*	$8.95

Also published by Resurrection Press

Discovering Your Light	*Margaret O'Brien*	$6.95
The Gift of the Dove	*Joan M. Jones, PCPA*	$3.95
Healing through the Mass	*Robert DeGrandis, SSJ*	$7.95
His Healing Touch	*Michael Buckley*	$7.95
Of Life and Love	*James P. Lisante*	$5.95
A Celebration of Life	*Anthony Padovano*	$7.95
Miracle in the Marketplace	*Henry Libersat*	$5.95
Give Them Shelter	*Michael Moran*	$6.95
Heart Business	*Dolores Torrell*	$6.95
A Path to Hope	*John Dillon*	$5.95
The Healing of the Religious Life	*Faricy/Blackborow*	$6.95
Transformed by Love	*Margaret Magdalen, CSMV*	$5.95
RVC Liturgical Series: The Liturgy of the Hours		$3.95
The Lector's Ministry		$3.95
Our Liturgy		$4.25
The Great Seasons		$3.95
Behold the Man	*Judy Marley, SFO*	$3.50
I Shall Be Raised Up		$2.25
From the Weaver's Loom	*Donald Hanson*	$7.95
In the Power of the Spirit	*Kevin Ranaghan*	$6.95
Lights in the Darkness	*Ave Clark, O.P.*	$8.95
Practicing the Prayer of Presence	*van Kaam/Muto*	$7.95
Stress and the Search for Happiness	*Muto/van Kaam*	$3.95

Resurrection Press books and cassettes are available in your local religious bookstore. If you want to be on our mailing list for our up-to-date announcements, please write or phone:

Resurrection Press
P.O. Box 248, Williston Park, NY 11596
1-800-89 BOOKS